Quick Relief for
Children's
Ministry
Leaders

by Ivy Beckwith

Group

Loveland, Colorado

Quick Relief for Children's Ministry Leaders

Copyright © 1998 Group Publishing, Inc.

Credits

Editor: Beth Rowland Wolf
Chief Creative Officer: Joani Schultz
Copy Editor: Candace McMahan
Art Director and Designer: Kari K. Monson
Cover Art Director: Jeff A. Storm
Computer Graphic Artist: Eris Klein
Cover Designer: SD&F Marketing Communications
Illustrators: Randy Glasbergen, John McPherson, and Ron Wheeler
Production Manager: Peggy Naylor

Library of Congress Cataloging-in-Publication Data
Beckwith, Ivy, 1954-
    Quick relief for children's ministry leaders / by Ivy Beckwith.
      p.   cm.
    ISBN: 0-7644-2072-0
    1. Christian education of children.   2. Christian education
directors.   I. Title.
    BV1475.2.B415   1998
    268'.432--dc21   98-12668
                                                      CIP

10 9 8 7 6 5 4 3 2   07 06 05 04 03
Printed in the United States of America.

Visit our Web site: www.grouppublishing.com

Contents

Introduction

Welcome to *Quick Relief for Children's Ministry Leaders!* Whether you're new to children's ministry or a veteran, you'll find lots of helpful tips and encouragement in these pages.

That's because the issues addressed in this book come from children's workers just like you. We chose the top sixty-four issues that readers of Children's Ministry Magazine have identified in reader surveys; then we asked Ivy Beckwith, a professional children's minister, to give us her best advice.

Ivy holds a doctorate in educational ministries from Trinity Evangelical Divinity School. She has served as the director of children's ministry at Wooddale Church in Eden Prairie, Minnesota, and she was children's pastor at Grace Chapel in Lexington, Massachusetts. Ivy speaks on the subject of children's ministry at conferences nationwide. She is currently a senior curriculum editor at Group Publishing.

In this book, you'll find helpful answers to your questions about working with volunteers, setting up programs, stretching your budget, and helping kids grow in Christ. You'll be encouraged, and you'll find new energy for your work.

You'll also find a one-hour training session to help you train and encourage your volunteer teachers. The training session is designed to be used with the companion book, *Quick Relief for Sunday School Teachers* (Group Publishing, 1998).

Take a few moments to glance through the questions in this book. We're sure you'll find several that catch your eye. It is our hope that this book will give you the help you need to make your ministry grow and thrive.

—The Publisher

Quick Relief
for Working With
Volunteers

How do I make sure new teachers know enough about the Christian faith and the Bible to teach children?

Sometimes it's tempting to be satisfied with just finding enough volunteers to staff all of your ministry's programs. But you can't afford to approach recruiting like that. Every ministry needs to develop guidelines describing appropriate volunteers. What volunteers know, live, and believe about faith and the Bible is perhaps the most important issue.

● **A relationship with Jesus.** It's imperative that your children's ministry teachers have a thriving faith relationship with Jesus Christ. Many churches require new teachers to be members of the church. This requirement helps ensure that your teachers believe what your church teaches. Other churches require volunteers to attend the church for six months to a year before they're invited to teach. This gives you a chance to observe and get to know potential volunteers before putting them into a position of teaching kids. During that time you will be able to discern the reality of the person's faith and the extent of his or her Bible knowledge.

● **Bible knowledge.** Volunteer teachers must have some Bible knowledge in order to teach kids the Bible, but they don't have to be Bible scholars. Most Sunday school curriculum can be taught by teachers with basic Bible knowledge.

Once a volunteer is in a teaching position, you can provide opportunities for him or her to learn more about the Bible and encourage participation in church programs or discipleship programs that encourage Christian growth. Start a sabbatical program for teachers. After they have taught for a certain length of time, give them time off to attend adult education.

● **Teaching ability.** Volunteer teachers must also have an idea of what it means to teach children. On your teacher application form, ask if the applicant has previous teaching experience. Make sure all your new teachers go through a new-teacher orientation that imparts basic facts about teaching children, the procedures and policies of your children's ministry, and job expectations.

How do I ensure that volunteers are teaching sound theological truth?

- **Church membership.** Churches that require their volunteer teachers to be church members help to ensure that their teachers believe what the church teaches. If you are unwilling to require membership of your teachers, you can require that they attend the membership class. This will help them understand the beliefs of your church and will help them discover whether they believe the same things.
- **Hold discussions.** Have a discussion with these potential volunteers after they've attended the membership class to see if they are in agreement with the teachings of your church. Before you meet with them, investigate what you and other leaders in your church consider the basic beliefs that all potential volunteers must agree with in order to serve.
- **Statement of faith.** In lieu of either of these suggestions, include your church's statement of faith with your teacher-information materials. In the volunteer's interview, discuss the statement of faith to see if he or she has any questions or areas of disagreement with it. Ask volunteers to sign the statement of faith as part of the application process.
- **Curriculum choices.** Choose a curriculum that is theologically sound and is in agreement with your church's teachings. If a volunteer teacher sticks with the lessons in the curriculum, there should be no problem. However, if you're worried about a teacher veering from the suggested lesson, spend some time observing that class and talking with the teacher about what he or she intends to teach.
- **Training times.** Spend time in teacher-training meetings talking about the beliefs of your church. Invite a pastor to talk to your volunteers about what your church believes. Allow time for questions. If you notice a teacher having a problem with a certain basic truth, talk privately to that teacher about it.

Help! Few people come to teacher training. How can I reach my teachers with training and new ideas?

Take heart. This is something we have all experienced at one time or another. Most children's ministry leaders have trouble getting teachers to attend training. Many volunteers are so busy they don't see the value in giving up precious hours to come to something they're not sure they need. But there are some things you can do to help teachers want to come to training meetings.

● *Make training a requirement.* Make sure that teachers understand that part of their commitment to volunteering to work with children is to attend teacher-training sessions. Help teachers understand that teacher training can help them do their jobs better and more efficiently. Teacher training can help teachers have more fun in the classroom, and it also gives volunteers a chance to meet wonderful Christians who share their interests.

● *Make meeting times convenient.* Ask your teachers when would be the best time to come to a meeting. Sometimes the best attended training meetings are scheduled when your teachers are already at the church. Consider holding a training meeting on a Sunday morning during the Sunday school hour. Provide a special activity such as a video, a party, or a Christmas ornament–making time for the children that morning, and invite parents to be the helpers. Provide your teachers a simple breakfast and some valuable training at the same time.

● *Evaluate the content of your meetings.* Volunteers need to see the benefit of training. They'll be more likely to attend if you can show that they'll walk away from the meeting with something valuable that will help them in their teaching. Know the issues your volunteers are dealing with, and plan your meetings around those issues. For example, if there are several children in your church with Attention Deficit Disorder, offer training on helping kids with this disorder. You might also consider combining training meetings with lesson preparation. Teachers will be more excited about meetings if the meetings help them save prep time rather than just being another time commitment that takes them away from their own families.

● *Consider alternatives to traditional teacher-training meetings.*

Start a monthly newsletter for your teachers, and include training tips. When you attend a conference, bring home tapes of the workshops to share with your teachers. When a Sunday school convention or one-day conference is in your area, invite your teachers to attend, and have the church pay their way. Start a lending library that includes videotapes, audiotapes, books, and magazines about teaching. Encourage your teachers to participate in this kind of independent study.

Also consider the one-on-one approach. Meet regularly with your teachers either individually or in age-level groups just to talk about what's happening in their classrooms. You'll be amazed at the amount of informal training that takes place in this kind of setting.

How do I prepare substitute teachers?

It works best to recruit a number of people who will be available as substitutes for an entire year. Treat substitute teachers the same way you treat your regular teaching staff. If you interview and screen teachers, do the same for substitute teachers. If you hold teacher-training meetings or an autumn orientation meeting, make sure substitute teachers are included.

● **Classroom visits.** If your substitute teachers are assigned to a certain age level, ask them to visit one of those classes at the beginning of the year so they have a chance to meet the children and understand the rhythm of the class sessions.

● **Clear expectations.** Make sure your substitute teachers know what to expect from being a substitute teacher. And make sure you understand what kind of commitment your substitutes are willing to make. Some are willing to substitute only if they aren't called too often; some are willing to be used whenever they're needed. Some substitute teachers value advance notice, and others don't mind stepping in at the last moment.

● **Share information.** Make sure your regular teachers understand any established policies on the use of substitute teachers. In addition, prepare a notebook or packet for each classroom that gives substitutes information about schedules, discipline policies, children's ministry policies, and the location of supplies. It's also important to provide information on the individual children in each class. Each classroom packet should include a list of the children who regularly attend. The list should include parents' names and other important information, such as children's food allergies. Finally, be sure to let substitutes know who they can turn to for help if they have questions or problems.

● **Use previous volunteers.** Former Sunday school teachers make great substitute teachers because they already know the ropes and can usually step right into a situation without too much orientation. When a teacher steps down from a teaching position, always ask if he or she would consider being a substitute teacher during the coming year.

What do I do when I need volunteers but there isn't anyone left to ask?

Before staring any campaign to recruit people to ministry positions, make sure you've begun by asking God to be with you and to work through you. Ask God to bring people to mind who might be able to fill open positions. Your ministry is really God's ministry. God has a plan for your ministry, so make sure you always ask God first.

● **Talk to the pastor and other leaders of your church.** Explain the scope and the needs of your ministry. Ask them to suggest people you may not have thought of or may not know. Enlist the help of your church's leadership in asking God to fill open positions.

● **Prayer support.** General announcements or requests for volunteers rarely work, but don't be bashful about appealing to

FINALLY, PASTOR SMITH'S WALL WAS COMPLETE WHEN HE
HEARD YET ANOTHER POTENTIAL VOLUNTEER SAY ...
"BUT I THOUGHT THAT'S WHAT WE PAID _YOU_ FOR!"

13

your church family to help pray for more volunteers.

● *Re-evaluate.* If you have truly asked everyone there is to ask (perhaps more than once), and you've been continually refused, perhaps it's time to re-evaluate the programs in your children's ministry. Are you trying to do too much for a church the size of yours? You may need to discontinue a program in order to have enough people to staff the other programs. Do this by setting priorities in your children's ministries. What are the essential programs? Do those, and discontinue the rest until you've worked out a staffing plan.

Maybe you need to try a different approach to staffing your programs. Maybe you're asking people to do too much. You might think about simplifying job descriptions. At first this may result in actually needing more people than you do now, but people are always more willing to volunteer when they know they can handle the job. You may end up with more volunteers than you need.

How Can I get more men involved in Children's ministry?

I t's a great idea to include more men in children's ministry. Kids need to be around men who are strong Christian role models.

But men, like anyone else, won't jump aboard a sinking ship. Men want to be involved in something that is on the move and important. So if you want men to be involved in your children's ministry, you need to be image conscious. How is your children's ministry perceived? To find this out, ask some men who aren't involved in the ministry how they perceive it. Then ask men who are involved in children's ministry why they chose to get involved. The answers to both these questions will be the catalyst for ideas to recruit more men.

● *Enlist the help of men's groups in your church.* Ask for time at their meetings to talk about children's ministry. Ask the leaders of these groups to challenge men to be involved in children's ministry. Challenging men to be involved in local church ministry is part of the ethos of some recent men's movements. Your pastor may also be able to suggest men who might enjoy working with children.

● **Use short-term commitments as a way for men to try out children's ministry.** Enlist men as volunteers for short-term events such as VBS. Try to hold some of these events in the evening. You'll find it much easier to increase your number of male volunteers when you hold VBS in the evening because men are more likely to have free time in the evening than during the day. In fact, holding events in the evening will greatly increase your pool of men *and* women volunteers. Intentionally recruit men to be involved in other special events for children, such as a fall kickoff night or a children's carnival. This gives them a taste of children's ministry without a long-term commitment. Keep track of men who seemed to enjoy the event, and put them on your recruiting list for next year.

● **Encourage the men who are working in children's ministry to recruit their friends.** When you make presentations about children's ministry to the church family, make sure you use lots of pictures of the men who are serving. Invite men to be part of these public presentations. Men are more likely to become involved when they see that they are needed and that other men are involved.

How can I get parents involved in children's ministry?

● **Hold open houses in the children's classrooms.** This will help parents understand what happens in children's ministry and what its needs are. Christmas is a natural time to do this. An open house also gives parents a chance to meet the teachers who work with their children.

● **Use parents as teachers and helpers.** You might enlist parents to teach or help in a class that is one age level above their children's current level. This kind of hands-on parent training will prepare them to understand their own children when the children reach that age.

Or you might slowly immerse parents in children's ministry by first asking them to serve as teachers' aides. In this way, parents get to "try on" children's ministry to see if it fits, and teachers get some much needed help. Similarly, parents can be used as small-group leaders in ministries with older children. These jobs require little preparation but can decrease the number of trained teachers needed to do everything in the classroom. After serving in these positions, parents are often willing to take on more responsibility in children's ministry.

● **Require involvement.** Another way to get parents involved is to require their involvement. Many churches do this in their infant and toddler nurseries. This is the least attractive way of involving parents and should be used only when all other means and ideas have been exhausted. It's much better to have volunteers who've chosen to serve than to have volunteers who've been required to serve. If you must require parents' involvement, do so on a rotating basis so that no one is required to serve all the time.

How do I keep volunteers coming back?

Volunteers continue to volunteer for causes they feel are important and to which they feel they're making a contribution. Keeping children's ministry volunteers is largely a matter of helping them to see the worthiness of working with children and helping them feel appreciated and valued in their ministries.

● **Spread the vision.** Help your volunteers understand what your church is trying to accomplish through children's ministry. Help them understand your vision for children's ministry and how their jobs help turn that vision into action. Continually keep the purpose of children's ministry in front of your volunteers, concretely linking it to the specific things they do each week for children.

● **Always treat your volunteers well.** Give them a lot of affirmation. Write notes commenting on something exciting you saw them doing with their children or their classroom. Surprise them with little gifts. (These don't have to be expensive. A caramel apple in the fall or a red carnation on Valentine's Day can do a lot to help a volunteer teacher feel appreciated.)

● **Clear expectations.** Make sure your volunteers know what is expected of them. Provide detailed job descriptions outlining expectations for attendance, preparation, training, and length of service. Make sure volunteers have what they need. Make sure supplies are readily available in their classrooms, and be willing to reimburse them for inexpensive purchases they make to enhance their class' experience. Do your best to provide classrooms that are attractive and conducive to working with children. Offer them time off, or give sabbaticals to volunteer teachers who have been faithfully teaching for several years.

● **Be available to your volunteers.** Stop in each classroom prior to the beginning of class to make sure teachers have everything they need. Let them know where you will be during class so they can find you if they have a problem. Stop by after class to see how things went and if there were any problems. Thank your volunteers often for all of their efforts.

● **Build a team ministry.** This helps people feel that they're part of something bigger than their class. Pair teachers as prayer partners, and encourage them to pray for each other's teaching responsibilities. Encourage teachers who work with the same or a similar age group to plan their class sessions together. Invite your volunteers to social activities that have nothing to do with teaching. If volunteers feel that they're part of a team and that the people they serve with are their friends, they will be more likely to continue in the same ministry year after year.

How do I train and supervise student helpers?

Older children and teenagers can be an excellent source of help in your ministry. The experience also gives them a chance to learn the basics of teaching while introducing them to service and participation in the church. Here are some ways to make it work.

● **Policies.** Develop a policy stating at what age and in what programs students may work as helpers. For example, you might not want to use junior high school students in the infant nursery, but they might be quite capable of working with the four- and five-year-olds. You will also want to consider when the programs for the helpers' age groups meet. Make sure your student helpers are not continually missing the worship service or their own Sunday school classes. Make sure the students have secured their parents' permission to be involved in this ministry.

● **Job descriptions.** Write a job description for your student helpers so they understand their role and exactly what is expected of them in the classroom. Define their duties, and be specific about requirements. Make sure the expectations are clear.

● **Train the helpers.** Offer mandatory training sessions several times a year for student helpers. Make sure the helpers have participated in this training before you allow them to help in any program. The training should be specialized for the age group the helper will be working with. For example, students planning to work in the toddler nursery should be made aware of the policies and procedures for the toddler area, students planning to work with first-graders should be aware of this age group's characteristics, and so forth.

Also include in the training an in-depth discussion of the job description. Sometimes teens see working in children's ministry as a way to get out of the worship service or their own Sunday school classes. Make sure they understand they'll be expected to be involved with the children. Encourage student helpers to ask questions about expectations.

● **Train the adults.** When student helpers are ready to be placed in the classroom, make sure the adults they're working with understand the helpers' role. Monitor their work through observation, conversations with the other adults in the room, and conversations with the student helpers.

● **Deal with any complaints or problems immediately.** Talk directly with the person who lodged the complaint, and talk directly with the student helper. With the student helper, develop a plan to prevent the problem from recurring, and discuss ways to implement the plan. If complaints and problems persist, have a plan ready for removing the student helper from the assignment.

How do I combat burnout, both my own and that of our church's volunteers?

et's talk about your own burnout first. Children's pastors and coordinators talk a lot about feeling burned out, but there are several things you can do to fend this off before it happens.

● **Guard your attitude.** One of the most important ways to stay enthusiastic about ministry is to guard your attitude. Remember that children's ministry is God's ministry, not yours. He has invited you to come along and be part of it, but he is in control. Consult him continually so you know his plans for the ministry. Don't forget to cast your anxieties on God—let him shoulder the

"DIRECT THE YOUTH CHOIR? UH... SURE, NO PROBLEM. WHAT? NO, GLAD TO DO IT! REALLY."

burden. You don't make ministry happen; he does.

● **Guard your time.** Whether you are a paid, full-time children's ministry leader, or a part-time volunteer leader, there are many practical things you can do to prevent burnout. Work on setting personal boundaries. You can say no to some requests. If you've planned to take a day off and one of your volunteers wants to meet with you that day, don't automatically cancel your day off. Explain your plans to be out of the office that day, and work together to find a time that is acceptable to both of you.

● **Time management.** Learn to manage your workload more effectively by attending a time-management seminar or reading one of the many books on this subject. Learn how to delegate. You may not be the right person to do everything you're doing. Could your secretary be doing some of the telephoning and clerical work you've been doing? Are you doing things for your volunteers that people on your leadership team should be doing?

● **Take time off.** Don't be a workaholic. Take your days off and all of your vacation time. Try not to deal with ministry issues during your time off. Let your answering machine screen calls. Spend your time off doing relaxing things.

● **Keep yourself spiritually nourished.** Make it a priority to attend the worship service. Join a small Bible study group (preferably one that has nothing to do with children's ministry). Don't forget to spend time alone with God.

Help for Volunteers

You can do several things to help your volunteers avoid burnout.

● **Be prepared.** Make sure volunteers always have what they need, whether it's supplies, reimbursements, or a listening ear.

Listen seriously to their concerns, and any time you can make a change for the better, do it. Constantly affirm your volunteers.

● **Guard their time.** Often you'll find that your best volunteers are also volunteering in many other ministries in your church—sometimes these people need a break. Be sure that you allow them to say no to new commitments. Never use guilt or manipulation to get a volunteer to agree to a request.

● **Give volunteers time off.** Be sure to honor the time commitments volunteers have made to your ministry. Also, help your volunteers stay spiritually nourished. Encourage them to attend worship and other adult education opportunities when they have a chance.

Some teachers shame and humiliate children as a means of discipline. How can I encourage more positive discipline techniques?

● **Discipline policies.** One way to avoid types of discipline that involve shame and humiliation is to institute a discipline policy and train teachers how to use it. Discipline policies inform teachers about acceptable discipline techniques. If you have a children's ministry committee or leadership team, work with this group to develop the policy. If you're in a smaller setting, work directly with teachers to develop discipline procedures. The discussions that take place will be enlightening to you and to the teachers as you work toward an understanding of appropriate behavior and discipline in your children's ministry.

● **Training times.** Use teacher-training times to talk with teachers about appropriate discipline procedures. Make sure teachers understand how important it is to always show love to a child even though they may abhor the child's actions. Encourage them to use words and phrases that convey love to the child. Talk with teachers about their own feelings of anger and frustration toward difficult children in their classes. Help them to find ways to like (and maybe eventually love) those children. Encourage teachers to keep a discipline log in which they note each child's behavior each week and how they handled it. Discuss the log and its implications with your teachers. You may also want to role play gentler, more effective means of discipline.

● **Watch closely.** If a teacher continually uses shame and humiliation with his or her class, action must be taken. Document your observations and the complaints you've received. Meet with the teacher and talk through the events. If the teacher is willing to make changes, agree on the changes, then monitor his or her progress. If the teacher is unwilling to make changes and doesn't understand the harm that shame and humiliation may do to the children, remove him or her from teaching.

How can I encourage spiritual growth in my volunteers and myself?

aking care of your own relationship with God is the most important thing you can do for your ministry. If your spiritual tank is empty, you'll be unable to support the volunteers, children, and parents in your programs. But it's easy for children's ministry professionals to find themselves running on empty. Urgent needs pull in many seemingly impossible directions, and time with God is often the one need that remains unattended.

● **Attend the worship service.** Ask God to clear your mind so you can focus clearly on God and what he has to say to you. So many children's ministers skip the worship service because there is always one more person to talk to or one more room to check. Sometimes it's more important to attend the worship service than it is to check a classroom.

Once you're in the worship service, concentrate on worship. As much as possible, don't think about the third-grade teacher who didn't show up or about what might be happening in the understaffed fours and fives room. Unless an emergency arises, stay in the worship service, remind yourself that God's in charge, and focus on giving yourself to God in worship for an hour. It will make a difference. Encourage your volunteers, especially your leaders, to attend worship services.

● **Take time during the week to spend alone time with God.** Spend time reading the Bible and just being with God. If you exercise during the week, use that time to talk to God. If you can manage it, plan retreat days that allow you a whole day away just to spend time with God. Encourage your volunteers to spend time with God. Model it for them through your behavior.

● **Ask for God's help.** Ask God to walk beside you through every conversation with a volunteer, through every conflict with another staff member, and through every recruiting call. Don't forget that ministry is really about teaching people how to have an intimate relationship with God. You need to be experiencing that relationship to effectively influence other people for Christ. Don't give up your own relationship with God in the hope of having more time to help others find that relationship.

How can I develop a strong children's ministry program when volunteers will only teach every other week?

Part-time teachers are a frustration to many who coordinate children's programs. Some churches have purposely chosen to staff their classes with part-time teachers, and it works well for them. But coordinators in other churches feel it's difficult to develop consistency in a program when volunteers are there only half the time. Here are some things you can do to develop consistency.

● **Make sure that volunteers who job share know each other.** This may sound like a no-brainer, but you would be surprised at the number of job sharers who are total strangers to each other. Encourage them to think of themselves as team teachers rather than job sharers. Those who team teach need to talk to each other about their class and their plans for it. Ideally they should plan together because this promotes consistency in their classroom. Job sharers and team teachers need to agree upon and enforce the same discipline policy so that kids know every week what is expected of them. If one plans a contest or a special event that runs more than one week, the other teacher should promote it and continue it. These things can happen only if the team teachers talk frequently to each other about their class.

● **Ask both teachers to be present in the class for the first few weeks.** This helps the kids to get to know both teachers at once. The teachers can explain their schedule to the class so the kids understand which teacher will be there in which month or week. This is especially important to younger children.

Consistency is most important for preschool and younger

elementary-age children. If you can recruit someone to be there every week, younger kids will feel more secure and the inconsistent attendance of the other teachers will not matter as much.

We're still three teachers short, and classes begin next week. What do I do?

● **Pray.** Continue to ask God to supply the volunteers you need. It is God's ministry, and ultimately he does the work. Trust God to supply everything you need. God's way may not look like what you had in mind, but it will perfectly take care of your needs.

● **Spread the word.** Talk to your pastor and other church leaders about people who might be interested in children's ministry. They may know of some likely candidates you are unaware of.

● **Stopgap measures.** You may have to put some short-term measures into effect. For example, you might ask a parent to teach the class for a month. This gives you a little more time to find a permanent teacher. Be sure, though, to live up to your end of the bargain. If you have not found a permanent teacher when the month is up, let the substitute teacher step away from the responsibility unless he or she wants to stay on.

● **Rethink your plan.** If you continue to have trouble finding volunteers for these positions, you may need to rethink the way you group your children's classes. Can some classes be grouped together temporarily? Can you reconfigure the way you group the age levels? Try to look at the problem in different ways. By viewing it only as a staffing problem, you are only looking for one solution: more volunteers. By looking for creative solutions, you might come up with an idea that could revolutionize your ministry.

How do I get volunteers to prepare their lessons in advance?

● **Forewarn teachers.** You should address the issue of preparation before a teacher is put into the classroom. The job description should explicitly spell out expectations for lesson preparation, and the teacher should be given an approximate idea of how long lesson preparation will take each week. This way, the teacher will go into teaching knowing that preparation is expected and knowing how much time it will require each week.

● **Help teachers see the benefits.** People will generally do something if they see it benefits them in some way. Show volunteers how preparation will help to them in the classroom. Explain that well-prepared teachers experience fewer discipline problems. Explain that teachers who come to their classes prepared are generally more able to engage the attention of their students. Well-prepared teachers are better teachers, and their students learn more. Prepared teachers are flexible teachers and are better able to meet the needs of the kids in their class.

Also, let volunteers know that their level of preparation communicates something about the importance of the Bible. If teachers view preparation of the Bible lesson as unimportant, then their students will learn that the Bible is unimportant.

● **Teach them how to prepare.** Some teachers don't prepare because they don't know how. Use teacher-training meetings or teacher orientation to give your volunteers the tools they need to prepare well. You can even use these teacher-training times to have the teachers look ahead and prepare future lessons by becoming familiar with the Bible stories, choosing activities, composing lists of necessary supplies, and noting where extra help or unusual preparation is needed.

● **Talk with teachers.** If advance preparation is a problem with only one or two teachers, take the time to talk to them individually about the problem. Find out why they are having a problem preparing their lessons. Ask them what you can do to help them. Point out the benefits of preparation, and develop a plan together to help them improve their preparation skills.

What goals are appropriate for children's ministry volunteers? How do I know that they're doing a good job?

Set measurable goals and expectations for your children's ministry volunteers. This makes it easy for you and for them to evaluate their performance. These goals and expectations should be officially spelled out in a job description. Here are some questions to ask:

Does the teacher
- show up for class when expected and on time?
- come to class with his or her lesson prepared?
- show evidence of building relationships with the kids in his or her class?
- ask for help when it's needed?
- provide a positive learning experience?
- usually maintain classroom order? (This will look different in each class.)
- provide an atmosphere conducive to children's spiritual growth?
- attend or participate in some form of teacher training during the year?

Do the kids in the teacher's class
- seem to enjoy being in the class?
- look engaged and interested during the lesson?
- know their teacher's name?
- seem to be learning something that is relevant to their lives?
- show little evidence of discipline problems?

You may come up with other questions, but this is a start. In order to evaluate a teacher, you must observe the teacher. Some churches also have teachers complete a self-evaluation form that addresses some of these questions. Then the teacher meets with the children's pastor to discuss the teacher's performance.

What should I do when a teacher isn't doing the job?

- **Make sure you have a standard by which to evaluate your teachers.** This should be a written job description outlining job responsibilities and expectations. All teachers should be given the job description before they are put in teaching positions.
- **Talk to the teacher.** If you have been hearing complaints about a teacher from parents or others who work in his or her area, take time to talk to the teacher about the problem. Always get the teacher's story. You may want to make time to

observe the teacher. If you observe that the teacher is not living up to expectations, document your observations, and talk to the teacher about the problem.

● **Investigate before you take action.** Don't assume that the teacher isn't able to do the job. Sometimes poor teaching stems from being improperly equipped or being unaware of all expectations. Have a friendly meeting with the teacher to find out why the job isn't being done and to determine what you can do to help the teacher meet the expectations of his or her job description.

● **Set goals.** If the teacher wants to do a better job and is open to coaching, then set goals for the teacher and monitor his or her performance over the next few weeks.

● **Consider removing the teacher from a direct teaching position.** If the teacher can't or won't live up to the stated expectations for the job, then he or she should probably be removed from the position. If this is necessary, be as tactful, warm, and helpful as possible. Don't forget to be considerate of the teacher's feelings. Remember that not everyone is gifted as a teacher. Some people are very conscious of the needs of your ministry. They love God, and they love children. They want to be supportive of children's ministry, and they may have agreed to teach even though teaching isn't their strength. Do your best to find these people supporting roles in your church's ministry. They might be more effective serving as organizers, supply buyers, game leaders, song leaders, or prayer supporters.

How can I get children's ministry volunteers to work together within a philosophy?

To be an effective children's minister, it helps to be a visionary who sees what the ministry can be, a developer who can design a plan for the ministry, and a salesperson who can bring others on board and encourage them to carry out the plan.

● **Develop a vision and a philosophy.** As you're forming your vision for ministry, meet with the church leadership and the volunteer leaders in your church to develop a good, overarching vision. Your vision is what you hope ultimately to accomplish through the entire work of the children's ministry at your church. You might want to concentrate on outreach, on discipleship, or on teaching kids that God loves them. Next, make your vision practical by developing a philosophy of ministry. Your philosophy of ministry will spell out in particular ways how your church will actualize your vision.

● **Get volunteers on board.** Once you've developed your philosophy, help your volunteers enthusiastically embrace your plan. Volunteers need to see more than the week-to-week business of teaching lessons; they need to glimpse the big picture—the exciting, dynamic children's ministry in its entirety and the changed lives that will result from their hard work and their willingness to stick to the plan.

Make your vision known by talking about it and keeping it in front of your volunteers. Put it on banners, buttons, self-stick note pads, and stationery. When you recruit volunteers, don't recruit them just for the little picture (the classes they will teach), but for the big picture as well.

Make sure the vision is articulated in ways your volunteers understand. The plan should be based on sound educational philosophy. But most children's ministry volunteers aren't professional educators, so avoid using educational jargon with them. Help them understand the "whys" of the philosophy, and help them to see results. Help them to see that kids really do learn when good educational philosophy is followed.

● **Build your team.** Another way to get teachers to work together is to help them feel that they're all on the same team. Plan social events and team-building activities at teacher-training meetings. Do all you can to help teachers know one another, like one another, and depend upon one another to excel in their ministries. Encourage your teachers to regularly show their appreciation for one another. Compliment the teachers, and encourage them to share examples with one another about how children's lives are being changed by their good work.

How do I encourage and affirm volunteers?

● **Be there for volunteers.** Be present on Sunday mornings or whenever their programs take place. Ask volunteers how they are doing. Ask them if they are encountering any problems you can help them with. Ask them if they need anything, and get it for them. Don't make them find you. Be accessible. **27**

● **Reward creativity.** If you see a volunteer teacher doing something fun or creative with kids, let him or her know. Write a note or drop in after class to tell the teacher what you observed. If parents tell you about something special a teacher did for a class, tell the teacher what the parents said.

● **Give gifts.** Surprise your volunteers with little appreciation gifts. They don't have to be expensive. A little surprise that says you love and appreciate a volunteer can go a long way toward lifting his or her spirits.

● **Give them what they need.** Make sure volunteers have enough curriculum pieces for their classes to make their teaching effective. Make sure craft, game, and media supplies are readily available. Tell volunteers at the beginning of the year what they may be reimbursed for, then reimburse them for any money they spend on their classes.

● **Tell the church about children's ministry news.** Comment on children's ministry events in your church newsletter. This gives visibility and importance to the children's ministry and helps volunteers feel they are participating in a ministry that is valued.

● **Give volunteers time off when appropriate.** Work hard to provide a working substitute list so volunteers don't feel they're tied to their ministry fifty-two weeks a year. Start a sabbatical program for long-term volunteers.

● **Invest in quality training.** Pay their way to a Sunday school convention or a local Christian education conference. Reimburse them for travel expenses. If the conference is in another city, pay for hotel expenses as well.

● **Work intentionally to create a team atmosphere in your children's ministry.** This helps your volunteers feel they are a part of something bigger than just their classes. A team helps volunteers feel supported by others who are involved in children's ministry. A team gives your volunteers others to share their frustrations and triumphs with.

How do I go about screening volunteers for safety checks?

Every church should screen children's ministry volunteers. Some churches complacently deny the need to do this because "we know everyone in our church" or "this is a small town; everyone knows everyone else." But many churches have been unpleasantly surprised when that church member they thought they knew has been found to have acted inappropriately with a child. No church, no matter how small, is exempt from the need to screen volunteers. Here are a few methods.

- **Church membership.** Some churches require potential volunteers to attend the church for six months to a year prior to serving in children's ministry. Some churches require membership for all volunteers.

- **Information forms.** Other churches require volunteers to fill out an information form. This form should deal with previous ministry experience, but it should also ask three things: Has the applicant ever been convicted of abusing a child? Has the applicant ever been abused? What are the names of references from previous ministries the applicant has participated in? If the applicant has been convicted of child abuse, he or she should never be allowed to work in your children's ministry. If the applicant has a history of being abused, you should have a long talk with this person because people who have been abused can become abusers. This personal history does not exempt the person from ministry, but it does raise a red flag for those recruiting for the ministry. Call the applicant's references, and simply ask what sort of experience the applicant has had working with children and if there is any reason the applicant should not be allowed to work with children.

- **Professional investigations.** Other churches contract with companies whose sole purpose is to do background checks for corporations. For a fee these companies will check with the police and the FBI to see if the applicant has a record of any criminal violations that would disqualify him or her from working with children. In some states, provinces, and communities, your local police or state police will do these checks for you.

- **How to handle resistance.** Plan to encounter some resistance when you announce your plans to screen volunteers. Some applicants will feel that you don't trust them and may refuse to work in your ministry if you screen them. However, it is important to stress that you are doing this for the safety of the children in your care and for the safety of the adults who care for them. For the most part, people will respond favorably to your plans to screen children's ministry volunteers.

Quick Relief
for
Programs
and Planning

Should I focus my time on the needs of kids already in the church or on bringing kids into the church?

It's easy to feel pulled in opposite directions with this issue. If you focus your time on the children who regularly attend your church, you may be missing an opportunity to introduce unchurched children to Christ. But if your focus is primarily on reaching unchurched children, you may miss the opportunity to help churched kids deepen their faith.

Your church's goals and priorities will help you set the goals and priorities for children's ministry. Consider the overall goals of your church. Is your church heavily into outreach? If so, bringing kids into your church is probably an expectation of your job.

What does your job description say? Is outreach to unchurched kids a condition of the job? If so, you'll know how to spend your time.

If your church holds no expectations for you and your ministries in the area of outreach, then you need to decide how to use your time. If you choose to spend a good percentage of your time on outreach events and with kids who are not from church families, make sure the church leadership is solidly behind this choice. Otherwise, church families may feel you're neglecting their children.

Make sure you are able to assimilate new children into your programs. Set up strong teaching programs such as Sunday school, Bible studies, and discipling programs. These programs will help deepen the faith of both newcomers and children who've always gone to church. If you don't do this, you'll end up with children who have only a superficial understanding of God and shallow commitments.

Another good strategy is to concentrate your energies on training the children in your church in outreach. Teach them how to share their faith with their friends, and help them learn how to invite their friends to programs at church.

How can I ensure that my programs and lessons are age-appropriate?

First, study age-appropriateness to make sure you understand it. An age-appropriate lesson includes activities that the child has the physical abilities to do. It also includes activities the child has the intellectual skills to accomplish. And the lesson deals with subject matter relevant and understandable to the child.

● *Know the characteristics.* As the children's pastor or coordinator, familiarize yourself with the specific characteristics of each age level. This will help you understand what a child can and cannot do at a certain age. If you have little or no understanding of age-level characteristics, a lot of resources can supply you with this information. Or you can take a child-development course at a local college to enhance your understanding of how kids grow. Another way to gain an understanding of age-level characteristics is to talk with education professionals in your church. Talk with preschool teachers, and observe preschoolers in action. This will give you valuable insights and information about what preschoolers are like. Make similar contacts with professionals working with other age levels.

● *Choose a good curriculum.* Choose an age-appropriate curriculum for your programs. Most curriculum publishers strive to make their products fit the particular age groups they are written for. Make sure age-appropriateness is one of your criteria in choosing a curriculum.

● *Train your teachers to understand age-appropriateness.* Make sure your teachers understand the age-level characteristics of the kids they work with. Include these in teacher-orientation materials, and use teacher training times to help your teachers understand what kids are like at each age.

Striving to make your programs age-appropriate is a great goal for your children's ministry. So many programs miss the mark with kids when they provide activities which may look fun but are not appropriate to the age group. A good way to tell if an activity is age-appropriate is to see if the activity frustrates the child. If a child has physical or intellectual difficulty doing the activity, it is probably not age-appropriate. Also activities may not be age-appropriate if kids seem bored with them or complete them in an uncommonly short period of time.

How can I create a fun program that isn't just fun and games?

Any program you create that is age-appropriate and engages kids will be fun. Sometimes adults make a stronger demarcation between serious and fun than children do. If kids feel valued, loved, and engaged, they'll have fun. That includes doing wild and crazy activities, but it can also include Bible study and discussion.

● **Age-appropriateness.** Kids become engaged in activities when the activities are age-appropriate. This means the activities are designed for the age group. A preschooler will become frustrated with an activity she can't do because of physical limitations dictated by her age. A fourth-grader will be bored by an activity that does not require him to use his developing intellectual skills.

● **Variety.** Children become engaged in activities that use a variety of teaching and learning methodologies. Children learn information in different ways. Using a variety of teaching methods will help kids deal with information in the way they learn best.

● **Active learning.** Kids become engaged in activities that require their active involvement. This may result in noise. Adults sometimes assume that if a children's classroom is noisy it must be out of control and the kids are learning nothing. This is not necessarily true. When kids are involved in active learning, the classroom will be noisy, and they will be learning.

● **A sense of worth.** Kids become engaged in activities when they feel valued, respected, and loved. How a church values children is seen in how the church views kids and how the teacher treats the kids in the classroom.

If you seek to include all of these characteristics in your children's programs, you will create a fun program that results in serious, real learning.

What should I do for summer programming?

First, decide your goals for summer programming. What do you want to accomplish with the kids in your church and community during the summer? Once you have determined that, you can decide the types of programs to offer.

"What to do with summer Sunday school?" is a question often posed to children's ministry coordinators. Consider both your volunteer resources and your overall teaching goals to help you determine how to handle Sunday school during the summer months. Many churches suspend Sunday school during the summer and change their worship options to accommodate more families in the worship service. Other churches continue Sunday school throughout the summer but significantly change the program. Some give their regular volunteer staff the summer off and recruit a new staff for the summer. Some change curriculum resources for the summer and make their age-level groups larger to require less staff. Some churches use a video curriculum for part of the summer.

● **VBS.** A staple in many churches' summer ministries is vacation Bible school. VBS is usually held for a week sometime during the summer. Some churches hold it in the morning, and others have turned to an evening VBS with good results. Many programs or curricula are available to meet the needs of all churches for VBS.

● **Backyard Bible clubs.** A variation of VBS that has also been successful for many churches is backyard Bible clubs. These are held in the backyards of church members throughout the summer. Children from the neighborhood are invited and involved in a five-day program with an emphasis on Bible learning. Many churches use these as neighborhood outreach programs. Curriculum specifically designed for backyard Bible clubs is available from Child Evangelism Fellowship. Most vacation Bible school curricula can be adapted to a backyard Bible club format.

● **Day camps.** Many churches hold day camps during the summer. These day camps range from generic camps that include field trips, games, and crafts to camps that revolve around specific themes such as sports, drama, or computers. These camps can be used for community outreach or to meet the needs of families and kids in your church.

● **Special weekly events.** A summer program that has been

successful for many churches is the one-day-a-week special event. With names like Terrific Tuesdays or Wild and Wonderful Wednesdays, these events take kids all over the community on special field trips. These special events are usually held during the day, but some churches have successfully held them in the evenings. Some churches spread out their vacation Bible school over the entire summer through these once-a-week events.

How should I plan the year? What's a good guide for how many activities to plan?

First, what do you and your church want to accomplish through your children's ministry this year? Spend some time deciding this before you even begin to think about programming for the year. Make sure the goals and objectives of your children's ministry are in step with the goals and objectives of your church. The balance in your programming comes from using these goals and objectives as your guide.

● *Determine your core programs.* These are programs you offer, no matter what your goals and objectives are. They could be Sunday school, children's church, midweek programs, and perhaps vacation Bible school. What you do in these programs should help to achieve your goals and objectives. Scrutinize these programs to see how well they help you achieve your goals and objectives for the year. Decide what you need to incorporate into these existing core programs to meet your goals and objectives.

● *Fill in the holes.* After shaping your core programs to help you accomplish your goals, find the holes in your programming. What still needs to be done that can't be done through the core programs? This helps you to see what programs to add to your children's ministry this year.

● *Consider the budget.* Will you have enough money to do everything you want to do? If not, prioritize your program needs. A program may be needed and it may be a really good idea, but it might not be essential to the coming year. Shelve the program, and plan to budget for it next year.

● *Volunteers.* Don't forget to take a realistic look at your people resources. Children's ministry coordinators are creative people and come up with hundreds of great ideas for programs and events, but sometimes the staffing necessary to implement those ideas outruns the available people resources. Ask if you have the people available to make the program successful. If not, maybe it needs to be put off until next year. Spend this year getting people excited about the idea so you have volunteers ready to go next year.

● **Coordinate with other church events.** Check your church calendar. Make sure a program you are planning doesn't conflict with something else your church is planning. Make sure all your programs and events are part of the church's master calendar.

It's time for our annual christmas pageant, and I'm not too enthusiastic. Do kids really benefit from these?

I t depends. Why are you doing these pageants? What do the kids understand to be the reasons for the pageants? Are they fun for the kids, or is a lot of emphasis put on a perfect performance? The answers to these questions will help to determine whether or not these pageants are beneficial to your kids.

● **Pageants help kids develop skills.** If handled properly, these programs can be a good opportunity for kids to develop faith-sharing skills, poise, and self-esteem. These skills are best developed if the director cares more about the kids than a perfect program. Also, kids should be allowed to be involved in more than just the performance. Involve kids in set building. Involve kids in the orchestral music, if appropriate. Let it be the kids' pageant, not an adult program that happens to involve some children.

● **Pageants spotlight the children's ministry.** Pageants provide good publicity and visibility for the children's ministry. Adults enjoy seeing children perform; often children's pageants are well-attended even by adults who don't have children in the program. Pageants and programs are a great way to make the rest of your church aware of the children's ministry at your church.

● **Pageants are also subtle outreach events.** Many unchurched family members will refuse to come to a worship service, but they will come to see a granddaughter or nephew in a Christmas pageant. Take advantage of the outreach potential inherent in these programs.

If directing a pageant is outside your area of expertise and talent, delegate it to someone who is comfortable with it. Or put together a pageant-ministry team in which each team member is responsible for a different part of the program. Some publishers offer "instant pageants" that require very little preparation but are fun and entertaining for both kids and adults. Check with your local Christian bookstore for these resources.

I have to choose a new curriculum. What do I do?

Choosing a new curriculum is a big job. Make it easier by thinking about these questions before you begin to evaluate various publishers' offerings:

● What do you want to teach?

● What do you want your kids to learn?

● Are there biblical and theological considerations that need to be included in any curriculum you choose?

● Do you want your curriculum to teach the Bible from a particular theological perspective?

● What kind of a teaching/learning philosophy is advocated in your programs?

● Do you want your kids to have a strong Bible-to-life application each week?

● Does your church expect you to stay with your denomination's curriculum?

● What is your budget?

● How big are your classes?

● How many teachers do you have, and how skilled are they?

● Do teachers or parents expect certain kinds of activities (such as a craft) or resources (such as a take-home paper) every week?

● What teaching equipment (VCR, CD player) is available?

After you answer these basic questions, you will have a good idea of what to look for in a curriculum.

Your next step is to get curriculum samples and information from all the publishers you are interested in. After you receive these samples, gather your children's ministry leaders and teachers to evaluate the samples according to your established criteria. While you are responsible for the final decision, it is important to get their input so you will have their support when the curriculum decision is made.

Look at each publisher's scope and sequence. This helps you to see the parts of the Bible the publisher thought were important to teach children. Check to see if the lessons and activities are age-appropriate. If possible give your teachers a chance to teach a lesson from the samples you are most interested in.

After this evaluation, call the publisher if you have more questions about a particular curriculum. All the Sunday school curriculum publishers have people on staff who know the product and can consult with you over the phone or in person. After this, choose the curriculum that best fits your established criteria.

After you have chosen a new curriculum, make sure you train your teachers in how to use it. Implementing the new curriculum will be far more successful if you take the time to do this. You can do the training yourself if you feel you are knowledgeable enough, or you can ask your chosen publisher to do the training for you.

Monitor teachers' use of the new curriculum to see how they are doing with it and to discover how they could be using it more effectively. Continue training as needed.

Take the time to carefully and wisely choose your church's curriculum. Ask lots of questions now because you will want to stay with your curriculum choice for quite a while. You shouldn't change curriculum every year or even every couple of years. That's because curriculum is designed to teach the Bible to children over the course of several years. If you change curriculum too frequently, children may repeat the same Bible stories again and again, and other Bible stories may never be presented.

How do I plan when there are three kids in first grade and twenty kids in second grade?

In planning class sizes and mixes, be flexible and sensitive to the fluctuating numbers of children in your programs.

● *You may need to change your plans every year.* One year

you may have enough fifth-graders to make their own class, and the next year you may need to create two classes that contain both fifth- and sixth-graders. Think ahead from year to year to determine what your needs will be. Just because you created your classes one way this year does not mean that is how you will do it next year. It all depends on the demographics of your church and community.

In this particular instance the ideal plan would be to create a first- and second-grade department, then create classes made up of both first- and second-graders. Most Sunday school materials are not closely graded, so most likely the materials you use for your first-graders are the same materials you use for your second-graders.

● **Be flexible.** Sometimes we get too hung up on age grading in our Sunday schools. Rather than trying to get the kids to fit our structures, we need to create structures that fit the kids. Some churches have even found that multi-age or multigenerational classrooms are the most beneficial to their kids. In a multi-age classroom, older kids are purposely paired with younger kids. The older kids learn by helping the little ones, and the little ones benefit from the example of the older kids. In multigenerational classrooms, adults and kids are placed in the same room. Many churches keep entire families together in the church classroom as an effective new way to do family ministry. The Sunday school teacher's role, then, is to help parents teach their own children.

Don't be afraid to consider different arrangements to see what will work best with the children you are ministering to.

I have to set up the whole program. How do I do it?

Setting up an entire children's ministry program is a lot of work. But unless you're at a brand-new church, chances are good that your church offered some sort of children's programming before you took on the leadership role.

Even if your church already has a children's program, pretend you're starting from scratch. Evaluate every program to make sure you want to continue it.

● **Gather information.** Talk to as many people as possible who have been in involved in the program. Find out what worked and what failed. Find out how people feel about the program. Are they frustrated? worn out? enthusiastic? willing to continue to volunteer? Find out what issues are important to the church body. Maybe your church is especially proud of the children's annual Christmas program, or perhaps the congregation in general feels that VBS is too much of a hassle to continue. The answers you get will help you know how to begin setting up a new program, and you'll also avoid making big gaffes that could make it difficult to get the congregation behind your new plans.

● **Meet with church leaders.** Meet with your church's leadership to determine what the church's vision is for children's ministry. Be sure to take the information you gathered when you interviewed children's workers., Discuss with the church leadership what your church wants to accomplish through children's ministry programs. Once you know where you are going, you will discover what to do in order to get there.

● **Choose programs.** The programs you implement will help you reach your vision. In a new church or one in which children's ministry has not been developed, your programs for the first year will probably revolve around Sunday morning and may include Sunday school and perhaps children's church. You may have other ideas of things you want to do, but it may be better to wait until you have core programs established.

If you are a newcomer to a church with an established ministry that needs to change, it may be best to maintain the status quo for at least a year before you make sweeping changes, especially if the established programs are going smoothly.

● **Consider your volunteer needs.** When planning the upcoming year, plan for each specific program you intend to implement. Determine your staff needs. How many people will

"THEN IT'S SETTLED! WE PAINT THE SUNDAY SCHOOL ROOM BLUE!"

you need to staff the programs? One way to determine this is by anticipating how many kids you expect to attend your programs during the first year. Use the preferred child-to-adult ratios (one adult to every five to six preschoolers and one adult to every eight to ten elementary-age children) to figure out how many volunteers you'll need. Also determine what your volunteers will do. Develop job descriptions that include specific information about what you want volunteers to do and how long their terms of service will be. Resources such as *No-Work Paperwork for Children's Ministry* (Group Publishing, 1996) can be a great help in setting up a good system for volunteers.

● **Choose a curriculum.** After you've looked at the big issues—your vision for children's ministry, what kinds of programs to run, and how many volunteers you'll need—then you must decide on particular ways to make your plan work. One of your biggest choices will be the curriculum you will use. Review your goals for your programs, and choose the curriculum that best helps you achieve them.

● **Policies.** You must also think about policies and procedures necessary to ensure that your programs are safe and welcoming to children.

● **Evaluate.** Last, evaluate your programs according to your goals. Did your programs accomplish what you had hoped? Did kids learn about God? Did things run smoothly? Did you create a safe and loving environment? Did you have the staff you needed to carry out your plans? How can you improve your plans next year?

Be specific and detailed as you plan and evaluate the children's ministry at your church. You'll find that the more you take care of upfront, the more effective the ministry will be.

How do I get children involved in worship?

There are two basic ways to approach worship for children. You can either keep the children with the adults for worship, or you can separate the children from the adults for all or part of the service.

● **Involving kids in adult worship.** If your church decides to keep kids with the adults, find ways to help parents help their kids understand adult worship. Encourage parents to talk through the worship program with their kids the night before. Many churches make their bulletins available by Friday afternoon or at least have the theme for the sermon printed in the church newsletter. With this knowledge, parents can prepare their kids before the worship service.

Before the service, parents can ask their children to listen for the answer to one specific question during the sermon. After the service, parents can talk with their kids about all that happened during the service. What interested the kids? What didn't they understand? What did they find boring?

Encourage your pastor and worship leader to make worship child-friendly. This may mean having a children's sermon or a children's worship bulletin. It may simply mean singing praise songs that kids know. Or it may mean finding ways to involve kids and families in leading the worship.

● *Involving kids in children's worship.* If you want to involve kids in children's worship, first decide what you want to accomplish through the program. Will your children's church be a teaching time in which kids learn about God, worship, and the church? Or will your children's church be a worship time in which kids actually experience worship at their own level? Maybe you'd like to achieve both of these goals. The answers to these questions will help you determine what kind of a program you offer and how kids are involved in their own worship at your church. Look for a curriculum that helps you involve kids in a worship experience that meets these predetermined goals.

Although it takes kids awhile to understand all that we mean when we talk of worship, they can participate in prayer. Make sure your children's church includes a prayer time. Kids of all ages can be very effective pray-ers. Teaching about prayer is a wonderful way to introduce kids to worship. Kids can sing, too. Singing is a great way to teach kids about praising God. Choose upbeat, kid-friendly songs that accurately teach about God. Your children's church should also include a short teaching time that reviews a Bible story, helps kids understand God, or explains some aspect of church life.

No matter how your church approaches children and worship, it's so important to teach children to enjoy worshiping God. Worship should be a joyful, rich experience for kids. Meaningful worship at a young age will help to draw kids into significant relationships with God, and it will set up a lifelong practice of church attendance and participation.

How do I connect kids with adults?

The best place for kids in your church to build relationships with adults is through established children's programs.

● **Connect kids with their teachers.** Sunday school teachers should see it as part of their job to build friendships with the kids in their classes. If they don't, write it into their job descriptions, and make sure when you recruit teachers that this is part of the discussion of job responsibilities. Adults who work with children in other programs should be held to the same expectation. Some midweek programs have ancillary programs for the express purpose of helping kids build relationships with other adults in the church. Investigate those to see if they would work for you.

Give your teachers and children's workers ideas about how to go about building relationships with kids. Show them ways they can do it during their class and program time, and make suggestions for "safe" events they might hold for their kids outside of class time.

● **Intergenerational learning.** Investigate the possibility of holding intergenerational learning events in your church. These events put children and adults together to learn the same subject matter. They work on projects together; they study the Bible together; they are in small discussion groups together. Intergenerational learning is a wonderful way for adults to get to know the kids in your church. These events can be as ambitious as a Sunday school class which meets for six to eight weeks or as simple as an event that happens on the fifth Sunday of the month.

● **Connect kids with older adults.** Some churches involve older adults with their kids by developing a surrogate grandparent program. This is especially useful if you have a lot of kids who live far from their grandparents.

● **Develop a mentoring program.** Mentoring is a hot topic. When an adult volunteers to mentor a child, the adult commits to spending one-on-one time with the child doing fun things, talking, and sharing his or her life. The concept is similar to the

Big Brother and Big Sister programs. This individual attention from an adult in the church can be a wonderful boost to a child. It can lift the child's self-esteem and be a positive influence in the child's spiritual development. Be cautious, though, in choosing your volunteers for a mentoring program for children. Because the adult will be spending time alone with the child, make sure that you have thoroughly screened the volunteer. This may mean calling references and running a criminal background check.

Many experts recommend that mentors and children meet at the church instead of one on one. By having everyone meet together, you ensure that children are not put in situations in which they may be mistreated. You also protect mentors from unfounded accusations.

Children in all churches benefit greatly from having close relationships with strong, growing, adult Christians. These relationships ground children in their faith. Watching an adult choose to live for God makes a strong impact on a child who's learning to make decisions independently. Children who have close ties with adults in the church are more likely to stay in the church as they grow up. Do whatever you can to foster deep friendships between the adults and children in your church.

Our church is near a school. Should I start an after-school program?

Just because your church is close to a school doesn't mean there is a need for a program of this type. Before you get too far into the planning, make sure you know that families in your community would use such a program. Talk with school administrators and community groups to determine the need for the program.

Then find out if your church leadership wants to do an after-school program. If the church leadership is not behind the proposal, then it will never happen.

● **Ask the tough questions.** After establishing support for this venture, refine your goals for the program. Do you want it to be an outreach to your community? Do you want to assimilate the kids who attend the after-school program into your church programs? Do you want it to be seen as a service your church body offers to the community? Do you want it to be all of these things?

● **Define the program.** After determining the program's purpose, decide what you intend this after-school program to be. Will it be an informal place for kids to come after school to do their homework, play games, and watch videos? Or will it be a more structured program? You might want to visit other after-school programs in your area for a sampling of the different types of programs you could offer. As you are defining the program, go through the proper channels at your church to determine what rooms in your building can be used and how much that will cost. Find out what other programs and groups use the rooms you would use to discover any areas of conflict.

● **Research government requirements.** Contact local and state governments to ascertain rules and regulations governing after-school programs. You may discover you need to renovate your church building before you can continue with your plans. These regulations will cover everything from building codes to who you can hire as staff.

● **Develop an action plan.** Once you've determined that you can comply with any licensing requirements, develop an action plan that outlines your specific plans for this program. Your action plan should include items such as developing a budget, hiring a staff, working with the community school, procuring supplies, and creating publicity.

Developing an after-school program can be a lot a work. But it can also be an invaluable service to your community, and it can serve as an effective outreach tool for your church.

How much teaching should there be in the nursery?

People who work in the church nursery need to see themselves as more than baby sitters. The caregivers who work with the youngest of children are teaching them something about God and the church simply by the way they care for them. If the needs of a very young child are met in the church nursery, the child will feel this is a safe place to be. Children will associate this sense of safety with the people who talk and sing to them about God.

● **Babies need quality care that includes some teaching about God.** The most important teaching going on in the church nursery comes from the care being given the children. But nursery caregivers can be intentional about teaching very young children. While changing a child's diaper, the caregiver can talk with the child about how God made his or her toes and fingers, sing a song about Jesus, or say a short rhyme or prayer with the child. Caregivers can also intentionally play Christian songs or lullabies in the infant nursery.

As kids grow into the crawling and toddler stage, more informal teaching can be done with them. As a caregiver sits on the floor playing with a child, the caregiver can introduce short activities that direct the child's thoughts to God and Jesus. As they look through books or at colorful bulletin boards together, the caregiver can talk about the things God made and how much God loves us.

● **Toddlers need more structured instruction.** Toddlers need some structured activity during the long Sunday morning. The people who are responsible for this age group can plan lessons around broad themes such as Creation and God's love. These lessons can include simple activities and songs centering around the theme. Remember that we teach toddlers when they are ready, not necessarily when we are ready. Those who care for toddlers should therefore be alert to moments when the toddlers are receptive to a finger play or another activity illustrating the theme of the unit. Don't expect toddlers to sit and listen for very long. Gather a group together, lead the children in a short song or activity, and then watch them wander off again.

Teaching in the nursery looks different from teaching other age groups, but it is still teaching. People who work in the nursery need to understand the importance of their jobs. They need to understand that young kids are always learning and that we waste valuable time in the nursery when we view our time there as only baby-sitting.

Money's really tight. How do I stretch my children's ministry budget?

Prioritize your program ministries. Are you trying to do too much for your church to support financially? If this is the case, decide what ministries for kids you really must offer, and cut back on some of the other programs until the financial picture improves.

● **What's your spending history?** Review your expenditures to see if you're spending the money you do have wisely. For example, do you buy your supplies (glue, scissors, and so forth) for the year from discount stores during back-to-school sales? When you need something for a program, do you comparison shop to discover who has the best price for what you need to buy? Have you told your volunteers what their budget is for their particular programs so they know how much money they have for the year?

● **Consider asking participants to pay.** While it is not a good idea to nickel-and-dime people for church programs, there are times you can ask participants to cover part of the cost of a program. For example, if you offer a midweek club program that uses handbooks, ask the kids to pay for part or all of their handbooks. Sometimes kids will value such things more because they've had to pay for them. Some churches charge a nominal fee for their vacation Bible schools in order to cover the cost of such items as craft materials.

● **Consider fund-raisers.** If your church allows fund-raisers, you might consider planning one to supplement your children's ministry budget. A variation on the traditional fund-raiser would be to hold a nursery shower for your infant nursery. Publish a list of the supplies you need, and invite the whole church to this special party. Stage it as if you were giving a baby shower, but instead of celebrating the birth of one baby, you are celebrating the births of all the babies in your church.

● **Research and plan carefully.** As you plan the next budget year, carefully research and explain your needs as you submit your budget to the church leadership. This will help the leadership understand exactly why you need the money you are asking for and why it is important they allocate this money to the children's ministry.

We have no space—help!

This is a common challenge in both small and large churches. Even those who've just come through a building program find they are out of space as soon as they have moved into their new building. Part of the problem stems from the fact that many times the people who make decisions about room allocation and building programs are not the same people who work with the children. These people don't adequately understand the space needs of kids. A good rule of thumb for figuring out space needs is to remember you need about thirty-five square feet for every preschooler and about twenty-five square feet for every elementary-age child. Now you feel even worse about your space problems, right?

● **Do a space audit, and reorganize where classes meet.** Maybe the available rooms in your church building are not being used to their greatest potential. Walk through your church building with your pastor or church leaders and note who uses each room and whether or not it's the best place for that group. Often adults get the best rooms in the church building simply because they are adults. This is not a good reason to give them those rooms. Children should have the most spacious rooms in the church because children need more room to move around in than adults do. After objectively auditing your church's classroom space, you may be able to move enough groups around to solve your space problems.

● **Consider adding another hour of teaching time.** If you don't have enough space to provide a safe, caring atmosphere for the children in your church, consider changing the times of your Sunday morning programs. For example, if you currently have a Sunday school program followed by the worship service, you consider having two worship services and running a Sunday school during each worship service.

If you have already chosen these options and are still out of space, it may be time for your church leadership to consider more radical alternatives such as a building program or starting a worship service and Sunday school on Saturday evenings.

Quick Relief for Working With **Kids and Families**

How do I encourage a heart for missions in children?

Teaching about missions can be tough because it's not a topic that's covered extensively in most curricula. But you can begin to incorporate missions education into your children's programs yourself.

● *Adopt a missionary.* Assign each Sunday school class a missionary to learn about as part of the class activities throughout the year. Encourage kids to write letters to the missionary, learn about the missionary's work and the country in which the missionary serves, and pray for the missionary.

If the missionary comes home during the project, arrange for him or her to visit the class and answer the children's questions in person. Make sure you give the missionary some guidance on how to make the presentation interesting to children. Nothing can dampen a child's growing enthusiasm for missions like a boring presentation from a missionary.

Don't be afraid to assign a missionary to your preschool classes. Young children are excited to learn about missions too. It may be helpful to assign your preschool kids a missionary family with preschool children. This gives the preschoolers a point of identification with the missionaries and their kids.

● *Missions-based VBS.* Vacation Bible school is a great opportunity to emphasize missions. Many churches select a missionary to spotlight during VBS. All week the kids learn about the work of that missionary, and sometimes an offering is collected to fund a special project for the missionary. Other churches choose a missions organization that sponsors a special project kids can participate in and spotlight the project throughout VBS week. Another VBS-related idea is to make the entire week a missions program in which every day the kids learn about missions, different countries, and the different jobs missionaries do.

● *Missions conference.* When your church holds its annual missions conference, plan a kids mission conference to go with it. Plan fun activities that help your children learn about missions in unforgettable ways. Involve your missions committee or board in the planning of this conference.

● *Missions and service projects.* It's important for children to learn about missionaries and the work they do, and it's also important for children to learn what it's like to do missions. Include your children in small missions or service projects. There's an appropriate missions project for every age group, even preschoolers. Young children can collect Bibles to give away, or they can sing "Jesus Loves Me" at a nursing home. Older children can be teachers' helpers in backyard Bible clubs, or they can serve meals at homeless shelters. Doing missions will help children learn to share their faith and to help others.

How can I encourage new families to come to my church?

Reaching out to new families should be a goal for your entire church; the children's ministry can't do it on its own. The church should develop an attitude of outreach so new families feel welcome.

Once the church has committed to reaching out to new families, there are many things your children's ministry can do to help achieve this goal.

● ***Hold a big event.*** Invite neighborhood children and their families to a nonthreatening event that enables families to comfortably learn about the church. Some churches hold harvest festivals in the fall instead of Halloween celebrations. Events like these are attractive to families who are concerned about letting their children go trick or treating. Have literature about your church programs available at the event.

● ***Use summer programs.*** These can be a great way to invite new families to your church. Vacation Bible school or backyard Bible clubs can be great draws for unchurched families. Target

THE BANFORD VALLEY CHURCH STOOPS TO RAW COMMERCIALISM
IN ITS ATTEMPT TO INCREASE ATTENDANCE.

neighborhoods close to your church, and blitz them with invitations to the events. Hold a closing program to which parents are invited. Have information about your church available, or make a video of your children's Sunday school to show at this program. Follow up on the kids who attend these events, and invite them to other programs at your church.

Day camps are another summer ministry that can be used as an outreach to families. Families, particularly those in which both parents work, are looking for programs to occupy their children during the day. Target families who don't attend your church as participants. Advertise your program in the late winter or early spring because this is when community day camps start to advertise.

● **Start a preschool.** Preschools or nursery schools are a good way to attract families to your church. These require a commitment by the church of both money and facilities, and they are subject to local and state regulations. But they can act as a strong magnet, attracting young families not only to your school but to your church as well.

● **Encourage children to invite their friends.** Teach the children in your church about outreach. Encourage them to invite their friends to various programs and then follow up with the families who visit. Meeting with a friendly representative from the church does a lot to show visiting families that your church cares.

How Can I involve Children with handicapping Conditions?

● **Accessibility.** The first step is to make sure your church building is accessible to children with disabilities. Are there wheelchair ramps and elevators? Are the doors wide enough to accommodate a wheelchair? Are the stalls in the restrooms wheelchair accessible?

● **Knowledge.** Look for people who attend your church who have experience working with people with disabilities. Ask them to do an assessment of your building's handicap access. Ask their advice in dealing with specific situations in your ministry.

● **Mainstreaming.** Look for ways children with disabilities can be mainstreamed into existing classes. For example, an interpreter could sit with a child with a hearing impairment. This would be a great learning experience for the other kids in the class as well.

- **Training.** Train your teachers to work with children who have disabilities. Many times teachers are reluctant to have children with disabilities in their class because the teachers are afraid they will do or say something wrong. Education can alleviate this fear. Have the parents of the child meet with the teacher. It might even be helpful to have the parents attend the class the first few times.

- **Special-needs classes.** If you have children with disabilities who can't be mainstreamed into regular classes, think about starting a special-needs class or program. Again, enlist the help of people in your church or community who have experience working with children with disabilities. Talk to people in other churches with similar programs. Find out what those churches do, and explore the possibilities for your church.

How do I minister to kids who are bused to church?

Children's pastors who work with bused kids offer several suggestions for working with these kids. First, any bus ministry has to have organization, structure, and a vision. The whole church, especially the senior pastor, must be behind your efforts, or the children will not be welcomed and the ministry will never achieve its goals.

- **Home visits.** Some ministries involve their bus drivers in visiting kids and their families during the week. These drivers also work in neighborhoods to find new families to be involved in the bus ministry. Churches find that these home visits help with discipline and classroom management when the kids are at church. The kids know that the church knows their parents and where they live. Often churches send birthday cards to children who attend their programs.

- **Flexible schedules.** Many churches with bus ministries hold Sunday school for the bused children on different days than they hold Sunday school for the other kids. These churches cite different behavioral needs as the reason for separating the programs. Those churches who integrate the bused kids with the regular church kids have the children attend morning worship services. These kids sit with volunteers during the service. **53**

● **High-energy programming.** Bus ministry workers stress the need for a high-energy program. A bus ministry program can have no dead time. Clear-cut behavioral boundaries are also essential. The kids need to know they are loved but that they won't be allowed to hurt themselves or anyone else.

How do I go about counseling kids?

Unless you are a trained counselor, you need to know your limits in the arena of counseling children. Children's pastors can certainly provide a listening ear to kids who are encountering problems. Part of your job should be to cultivate an environment in which kids feel comfortable coming and talking to you. However, kids may come to you with deeper problems than you are equipped to deal with—problems such as abuse, mental illness, or thoughts of suicide. You need to know when to alert parents. You need to know when the problem is too big for you to handle and when to refer the family to a trained professional. You also need to know your state's laws regarding your role as a mandated reporter. Some state laws require church workers to report any instances of abuse that they know about or suspect.

Bearing all that in mind, here are several ways to convey to children that you are a safe person and that they can come to you with their problems.

● **Get to know the kids.** First, be physically present to children. If kids know you, they will be more likely to talk with you when they encounter a difficulty. Kids need to see you as a person who will listen. Pay attention when kids talk to you, and this will establish your credibility as a listening person in their minds.

● **Respect confidentiality.** Sometimes kids are unwilling to talk unless they are assured you won't tell anyone. For the most part, you may promise to keep confidentialities with the kids in your church. But also tell them that you won't keep secrets when the situation they tell you about might hurt them or someone else.

● **Talk to kids about God.** Also remember that you may in a way represent God to the kids who come to you with a problem. This gives you a wonderful opportunity to address faith issues with them.

● **Be an advocate.** You can sometimes play the role of

advocate in a child's life. By establishing an atmosphere in which kids feel safe talking to you, you may be able to protect a child when few others will.

● **Support groups.** Programs exist to help you set up support groups for kids dealing with a variety of difficulties. For example, you can find specific curricula or programs for children dealing with divorce, a death in the family, a parent's illness, a move, or a parent's job change. These support groups offer kids a safe place to talk about their feelings and offer them life skills to cope with the emotional disturbances that come from personal crises.

What do we do with sixth-graders—especially the boys?

Most churches place sixth-graders in the same way that the local school system places them. If the local school system continues to place sixth-graders in elementary schools, then most churches continue to place them in the children's area. If the local school system places sixth-graders in middle school, many churches then place them in their junior high programs. Sometimes this presents a problem because a sixth-grader and an eighth-grader are very different. Churches may combat this problem by creating an in-between kind of program for sixth-graders. This works if you have enough sixth-graders to form an enjoyable group size.

If you continue to include sixth-graders in your children's ministry, there are several things to remember about them.

"I THINK WHAT MRS. NITWHIPPLE IS TRYING TO SAY IS THAT WE NEED HELP WITH THE SIXTH-GRADERS THIS MORNING."

- **Sixth-graders want their own activities.** They will not want to participate in any activity younger kids participate in. You may have planned the best and most fun activity that's ever been planned, but if the younger kids are doing it, the sixth-graders will remain uninterested. Sixth-graders generally need their own programs and meetings.
- **Sixth-graders are socially sophisticated.** They know a lot about the world, and at times it is difficult to see how they differ from a junior high student. But they are different in the area of emotional development. In many ways sixth-graders are still children. We must never forget this when we work with them.
- **Sixth-graders are demanding.** A teacher who puts little preparation into his or her lesson will have a hard time with sixth-graders. They come to class prepared to be bored. But if they are engaged through thoughtful and active methodologies, they will respond.
- **Sixth-graders are searching for spiritual answers.** Sixth-graders have reached a stage in their intellectual development where they don't automatically believe the stories they learned in Sunday school anymore. They need adults who will respectfully listen to their questions and help them work toward the answers.
- **A word about the boys.** Discipline seems to be the big issue for teachers of sixth-grade boys. They are lively, sometimes disrespectful, sometimes silly. To be effective, any teacher of sixth-grade boys must show respect for the boys and their interests and work on building a relationship with each boy in the class. But the boys need to know their limits. The teacher must let them know his or her expectations for their behavior and then hold them to those expectations.

Sixth-graders can be exasperating and tiring to teach. But this group is exciting, too. Sixth-graders are old enough to allow you to glimpse what they'll be like as adults. They're beginning to reason for themselves and reaching a point where they'll own their faith and act on it in a way that younger children can't. Sixth-grade teachers have the privilege of helping young adolescents cross over from a child's simplistic faith to an adult's thought-out faith. It can be a richly rewarding experience for teachers.

How do I equip parents to teach their children about faith at home?

According to the Bible, the home is to be the primary place for a child's spiritual nurturing. The church should do all it can to help parents reclaim this responsibility.

● **Inform parents.** Start by informing parents of their children's activities in Sunday school and other children's programs. You'd be surprised how many parents don't know their children's Sunday school teachers or are unaware of the goals of your children's ministry. Hold open houses and parent meetings at the beginning of the school year to educate parents about what is happening in children's ministry. Encourage parents to use the church's take-home papers throughout the week to reinforce Sunday school lessons. Encourage parents to ask their children for any papers that come home from church. This will help ensure that take-home papers actually make it home. If you have a memorization program in your Sunday school, mail the verses to parents at the beginning of each quarter so they can work on the verses with their children.

● **Newsletters.** Consider developing a monthly or quarterly family newsletter that includes information about what the children are studying in their programs. Include suggestions for family activities that help to reinforce the lessons and the real-life applications. Suggest ways for families to talk about spiritual matters together. Many books are available to help parents incorporate activities in everyday life that teach about God. Stock your church library with books such as *The Pray & Play Bible for Young Children* (Group Publishing, 1997) and *Fun Excuses to Talk About God* (Group Publishing, 1997). Be sure to let parents know that your church has these resources.

● **Parent training.** Offer parents training in how to talk with their kids about spiritual topics. Parents want to do this but often don't know how, so they don't do it at all. Help them see that spiritual nurturing grows informally out of the everyday activities of life. Above all, be encouraging and available to parents who want to know more about teaching their children.

How do I support parents of troubled kids?

● **Develop relationships with kids and parents.** The first and most important thing you can do is to develop relationships with the parents of the kids in your ministry. Let them see you as a support person and an advocate. If you develop these relationships, then parents will feel comfortable coming to talk with you when trouble does happen. The most important thing you can do for parents of troubled kids is to listen to them. Unless you are a trained counselor or psychotherapist, you should not attempt to give parents of troubled children psychiatric counseling. Give them a listening ear. Offer them spiritual counsel. Support their attempts to work with their children. Refer them to professional counselors if necessary.

● **Develop a support group.** If you have any professional counselors in your church, talk to them to find out what would be involved in developing a support group for parents of troubled kids. These would not be therapy groups but a place for parents to talk about their problems with their kids. They would meet others who might be experiencing the same difficulties and perhaps share ideas and strategies.

● **Offer parenting helps.** You might also want to think about proactive strategies for parents. Offer parenting classes. Help parents learn how to be good parents, and perhaps this will help to prevent problems.

How does divorce affect what I do in Children's ministry, and what should I do about it?

Divorce affects children's ministry programming in several ways.

● **Some children won't be at church every Sunday.** When children are in the custody of parents who are living apart, they often spend weekends with the noncustodial parent. This means that the child will probably not be in your Sunday school every week. This has implications for the structure of the lessons and for projects done in Sunday school classes. If a teacher plans a project to be completed in two weeks, it could mean that half the class won't be there to start it and the other half of the class won't be there to finish it.

● **Be aware of possible behavior problems.** Children whose parents are divorcing are often confused and angry about what is happening to their family. They may act out their emotions through inappropriate behavior.

● **Money is tight.** Single mothers and their children often have a lower standard of living than average. This may have implications for the types of events you hold in your children's ministry. Families with more than one child may not be able to pay for program handbooks or special events.

● **Be sensitive during holidays.** Having kids from divorced families in your church will affect the way you talk about holidays such as Mother's Day and Father's Day. We can no longer assume that every child has a mother and father living at home. If it's been your custom to hold such events as father-daughter banquets, you may need to rethink them.

● **Safety issues.** Safety procedures become an issue when you are working with kids from divorced families. Custody issues are often heated and emotionally bloody. Churches without fully enforced check-in and check-out procedures for children are prime targets for child-snatching in a custody battle.

These are all issues to consider if you are working with a lot of kids from divorced families. The more of these kids you have in your programs, the more it will change what you do in children's ministry.

How can I support blended families?

Blended families are tricky business. In ministry, just being sensitive to the amazing complexities of the blended family is half the battle.

● **New family dynamics.** For elementary-age children, becoming part of another family and having new brothers and sisters can be traumatic. Kids also have to deal with sharing a parent with the children in the parent's new family. These transitions can cause anger, resentment, and confusion in all of the children.

For parents the blending of families means learning to parent other people's children or watching their own children be parented by someone else.

In the blended family, conflict can arise over discipline,

sharing of resources, ex-spouses, family traditions, and a myriad of other issues.

● **Sharing custody.** Parents who share custody must cope with kids being part of the family for part of the week only. And if the new spouse also shares custody with an ex-spouse, then the makeup of the family can be different every day of the week. Just keeping schedules straight can be a full-time job. If this is difficult for the parents, imagine how the kids feel as they are thrust into different homes and different parenting situations. Kids may also be unable to attend the church's programs regularly. Be sensitive to the fact that kids may not be able to attend every week. Don't plan activities and lessons that assume regular attendance.

● **Consider offering a class.** Some churches offer courses on helping families make the transition to blended families. These courses last four to six weeks and deal with the issues of blended families and how to cope with them. Other churches develop support groups for parents involved in blended families. These groups give couples a chance to talk about their families while other couples who have dealt with the same dynamics offer insights into coping with the difficulties.

Is it OK for children to do fund raising at church?

This all depends on how your church views the subject of fund raising. Some churches prohibit any kind of fund raising because they feel it is wrong to sell things to raise money for the church. These churches rely on the free gifts and offerings of their members and their attendees to support the monetary needs of the church's ministry. If this is the stance of your church, then your kids should not be allowed to do fund raising.

If your church is accustomed to fund-raising programs, then it is probably OK for the children's ministry to be involved in them. But there are some cautions. If you want the kids to actually do the fund raising, then you must decide at what age this is appropriate and what type of fund raising is appropriate.

● **Fund-raiser overload.** Remember that kids and parents are bombarded by schools and other civic organizations with fund-raising projects. They may not appreciate another project requiring their kids to sell something to raise money for the church

(where they may already give money freely).

● **Liability issues.** You should also consider liability issues before you undertake a fund-raising project. For example, before your sixth-graders hold a carwash, check with your church's insurers to make sure you're protected if someone's car is damaged.

● **Consider donations.** Sometimes better projects for children's ministry are those that invite church members to donate supplies or money toward a special purchase. You might want to think about projects that involve both kids an adults. For example, if you hold a fall festival, include several activities that have a cost attached. Explain that any donations received from those activities will fund a specific event or project for the children of the church.

What do I need to know about keeping kids safe?

Here are some ways to make your church building and campus safe places for kids.

● **Check the nursery.** Start in your nursery. Are the carpets and floors cleaned regularly? Is the furniture in good repair? Are the toys washed regularly, and have all choking hazards been removed? Are the cribs and other equipment in good repair and safe for infants and young children to use? Look closely for anything that has the potential to harm a child.

● **Inspect classrooms.** Is the furniture in the preschool classrooms sturdy? Are the toys in good repair? Are all cleaning solutions locked away from children or out of reach? Is the furniture the appropriate size for the age group?

● **Check the outside of your church building.** Is playground equipment in good repair and cushioned by material recommended by your state licensing authorities? Are kids properly supervised when using the playground equipment? Do you have policies about using the playground equipment that your volunteers know and follow?

● **Develop safety procedures.** Make sure you have a policy about safety procedures and practices. Inform your volunteers of these, and make sure they practice them. For example, do your nursery volunteers always wash their hands after changing a diaper? If not, they could be spreading disease throughout the nursery. Have you posted evacuation routes in case of fire or natural disaster in all of the classrooms? Are volunteers and parents aware of these procedures? Do your volunteers know what to do in case of an accident involving a child?

- **Institute a check-in program.** Have you instituted a check-in program for your nursery and preschool ministries? Many churches give parents a tag when they bring their children into the classroom, and the parents must then present the tag in order to retrieve the child. This system helps to ensure that young children are not being given to people who should not have them.

- **Investigate volunteers.** You must be careful about who you choose to work with children. Do you have policies about who can work with children? Do you interview these people and check their references? Do you have policies about the number of adults required to be in a room with children? Have you established policies about taking children to the restroom and what kinds of touch are appropriate? Do your volunteers understand these policies and abide by them?

If you can answer "yes" to most of the questions posed here, you are doing a good job of keeping children safe. If most of your answers are "no," then you need to work on developing policies and procedures that will help to make your church a safe and friendly place for children.

What are my responsibilities if I suspect a child is being abused?

- **Know what your state requires.** Your legal responsibilities depend on the laws of the state or province in which you live. Many states have designated people in certain professions as mandated reporters. These professions generally include schoolteachers and day-care providers, but some states include clergy or church workers in their definition of a mandated reporter. If you are designated a mandated reporter, then you are required by law to report any known or suspected abuse of a child to the appropriate authorities. It is important to know your state's laws in this area. Not knowing your status as a mandated reporter is not an excuse for not reporting known or suspected child abuse.

- **Develop a church policy.** But beyond what the law says, your church should have a policy for dealing with known or suspected abuse of a child in the care of your ministry. Make sure the volunteers in your ministry know what to do and who to go to if they know or suspect a child is being abused. Address this issue in writing and in any orientation meetings you hold for volunteers. Then, if you are required by law to report this to the appropriate authorities, someone in the church should be designated to do so. Once these procedures are established, make sure everyone is willing to use them. In some states you and your church can be found liable for not reporting suspected abuse. Beyond the liability issue, we want our churches to be safe places for children. Protecting them from people who seek to hurt them is one way to create a safe environment.

How can I minister to abused kids?

It is unfortunate that children's pastors have to ask this question. But in reality, everyone who works with children in the church will eventually have to deal with an abused child.

First, understand how abused children are feeling and how they view their world. They are fearful. The world has become an unsafe place for them. Abused children have a skewed view of love. Because the people who were supposed to love them have hurt them, they associate love with pain. Abused children think they are responsible for the abuse. They think they must have done something wrong, that they deserve the abuse. The abused child becomes a survivor and often tries, at all costs, to keep the family together in spite of the abuse.

In "Abused Children," a chapter of the book *When Children Suffer*, Virginia D. Ratliff and J. Bill Ratliff offer some guidelines for those who attempt to minister to abused children.

● Treat the child with kindness, as you would treat other children.

● Show respect by speaking to the child at eye level. This helps the child not to feel overpowered by another adult.

● Take your time when asking the child to talk about the abuse. When the child chooses to tell you about the abusive experiences, listen.

● Encourage the child to feel free to talk to you whenever he or she wishes.

● Remember that in most states you are required to report suspected abuse to the appropriate authorities. Make sure you know what your state laws are in regard to this issue.

Quick Relief
for
Ministers

How do I know if I'm doing children's ministry right?

No formula exists to tell you if you're doing children's ministry right. But you can gauge the success of a children's ministry by a number of factors.

- **Have you met your goals and objectives?** First, are you meeting the goals and objectives you've set for the ministry? Is your vision for the ministry being accomplished? If the answer to these questions is "yes," and if the goals and objectives are worthy children's ministry goals, then you are probably doing children's ministry right. If your answer to these questions is "sometimes" (and this is what most children's pastors would answer), then you need to evaluate the areas of concern. Perhaps the goals you've set are not realistic, or maybe you haven't given yourself enough time to accomplish them. Or maybe other things came up, and you just didn't have the time to work on a particular goal. This is all OK and doesn't mean you've failed at children's ministry. Just continue to plan for what you want to do, and continue to evaluate what you are doing.

- **Do volunteers stay connected to the programs?** Ask other evaluative questions to see how you are doing. How many teachers do you retain each year? If this number is a high percentage of the total number, then you are probably doing a good job of working with your volunteers. If the percentage of the total number is low, ask why. Sometimes teachers don't return to teaching for reasons that have nothing to do with your volunteer-management skills. They have babies. They move. Their kids move into the junior high program. But sometimes there are things you can do to keep volunteers returning year after year. Find out what you can do to make volunteering a better experience.

- **Do kids enjoy the programs?** Do kids enjoy being involved in the children's programs at your church? To answer this question, observe kids during class. Do they look bored or interested? Ask their parents what their kids say to them about the programs. Or ask the kids themselves what they like and don't like about the children's programs. If you discover a lot of bored kids, change directions to make sure kids are always actively involved.

- **Are kids growing in God?** Also look for evidence that the kids in your programs are developing relationships with God.

Are the kids treating each other with kindness? Are they eager to learn about God? Are they interested in the Bible? Are they involved in helping others? What do the parents and teachers tell you about the children's relationships with God?

In many churches, evaluation is a formal, once-a-year process in which each program is critiqued. But it's important to informally evaluate your ministry constantly. Be ready to change what doesn't work, and be sure to celebrate successes.

I want to minister, but mostly I manage and administrate. How can I feel like I really am making a difference?

You wanted to work in children's ministry because you love kids, and now you've discovered that you never get a chance to be with the kids because you spend all your time recruiting volunteers and ordering curriculum. This is a common scenario. Many people go into children's ministry thinking their role will be that of an elementary school classroom teacher and find, instead, they are playing the role of the principal. But don't ever think that by playing the role of principal and administrator you aren't ministering.

● *Administration is part of your ministry.* For children's ministry to succeed, administrative skills are required. Teachers must be recruited, goals must be set, letters must be written, and meetings must be attended. Please do not view these administrative tasks as anything less than ministry. Without this backbone of organization, ministry to kids would never happen in your church's programs. By learning and using administrative skills, you are making a difference in kids' lives.

If by nature you are not administratively inclined, you need to do two things if you intend to stay in children's ministry. First, learn some rudimentary administrative skills. Bookstores are overflowing with books about goal setting, time management, and people management. Read some of them, and begin to practice the skills they preach. Second, surround yourself with organized people. When you recruit a vacation Bible school director, seek someone with strong administrative skills.

● *Carve out time to be with kids.* Even though much of the

children's coordinator's time is spent on administrative detail, this does not mean you'll never have a chance to be with kids. You have to be intentional about it. You can still participate actively with kids, but you need to carefully choose when and where you will be involved. You may choose to be the regular substitute for a class or the coordinator for summer day camps. These are short-term assignments, but they still give you the opportunity to love kids and exercise your skills in working with them.

You may not often find time to be in the classroom, but you can still develop relationships with kids. Make an effort to learn their names, and ask them how their week went. Offer to pray with and for kids, and then be sure to do it. Encourage children by noticing how they're growing in God. Send them notes; compliment them to their parents; find places for them to serve.

● **Part of your ministry is to adult volunteers.** Another area of ministry that you may not have thought of is your relationship with volunteers. Your encouragement, training, prayer, and friendship will help the adults who work in children's ministry grow in their spiritual lives. Start to consider adult volunteers as part of your ministry. Do everything you can to encourage workers to know, love, and follow Christ. Doing this will make your children's ministry more effective.

Children's work is more than a job; it's a ministry. How do I cultivate a servant's heart?

You've hit on one of the major ambiguities that everyone who has a ministry job faces. On the one hand, you may receive a paycheck for doing the job called children's ministry. You hold somewhat regular hours and go to an office, just like everyone else who has a job. But there is a difference. Your job has spiritual and eternal consequences, and all over the world there are people who do the same job you do for no paycheck. So how do you meld the two and hold a proper attitude toward the job and the ministry?

Remember that this is something God's called you to do. God works through you to bring children into meaningful relationship with him. God has invited you to come along with him on this adventure. Developing a servant's heart is easier when you remember that the ministry belongs to God.

● **Spiritual health.** In order to do this, make sure you remain spiritually filled. The quickest route to burnout is to neglect your own spiritual nurturing. Many children's pastors never make it to the worship service because they have too many things to do and too many people to see. However, spending time with God is the only way to keep a correct focus while doing something as demanding as children's ministry.

● **Guard against bad attitudes.** Sometimes bad attitudes creep into the world of the children's ministry leader. You didn't get the budget you requested, or you have trouble recruiting volunteers for a ministry you consider really important. You can become jealous or afraid, and you can forget that God is in charge. Bad attitudes can cause you to forget you are serving God and begin to see children's ministry as just a job. Staying close to God is the remedy for bad attitudes.

● **Find a support person.** Find a friend or prayer partner, preferably someone not involved in children's ministry. Use this person as a sounding board and as a barometer. Ask this person to help you stay on track in terms of your attitude and sense of personal servanthood.

I need help—resources, support, ideas—where do I go?

● **Local fellowships.** Check with other children's leaders in your area to see if there is a local fellowship of children's leaders. If there is, start attending. These groups are wonderful places to share ideas, resources, and problems. If nothing like this exists in your area, get together regularly with other people in children's ministry to share resources and support one another.

● **Denominational specialists.** Your denomination may have a Christian education specialist whose job is to support people like you in the local church. Call the local denominational office to see if such a person exists in your area.

● **Bookstore representatives.** If there is a Christian bookstore in your area, make friends with the person who buys the curricula and church education resources. This will keep you informed of the latest products from Christian publishers. Often bookstores hold teacher- and leader-training workshops. Ask if your bookstore ever plans to sponsor such an event.

● **Publishers.** The publisher of your Sunday school curriculum may be willing to send a Christian education consultant to visit with you to discuss your ministry's needs. These consultants can help train your teachers to use their materials as well as offer helpful suggestions in other areas of teaching.

● **Conferences and conventions.** Local Sunday school conferences or conventions are held in most areas of the country. Check with church leaders in your area for the dates of one near you. These conferences offer workshops on a lot of different topics related to church ministry. Also, they usually exhibit valuable ministry resources. Some publishers and nonprofit children's ministry groups hold one-day seminars all across the country. Watch for information on these, and plan to attend.

Subscribe to a magazine, such as Children's Ministry Magazine. This will give you a lot of ideas you can use right away.

I never studied children's ministry. Is there a list of the top-ten books I could read to learn to do this job?

There are many great books on children's ministry. It would be almost impossible to narrow it down to the ten best books. Instead, here is a list of the types of books you should read and where to find them.

● **Child development.** Read one good book on child development. You can find these in the "family and child-care" or the "psychology" section of your local bookstore. This book will help you to understand how children grow and develop at various stages of their lives.

● **Education.** Read books on teaching children. These can be found in the "education" section of your local bookstore.

● **Organization and administration.** Look for books on organizational management. Because much of your job as a children's pastor is administrative, you should be familiar with management styles and techniques. You can find this type of book in the "business" or "management" section of your local bookstore.

● **Christian education.** Read books devoted exclusively to

Christian education and to the spiritual nurturing of children. These books fall into two categories: theoretical and practical resources. The theoretical books will help you understand how to help children grow spiritually through applying developmental theory and how to specifically manage and administer Christian education programs. Such books are published by Moody Press, Zondervan Publishing House, Broadman and Holman Publishers, and Religious Education Press. Your local Christian bookstore may have some of these books, and if you live near a Bible college or seminary, its bookstore would also carry some of these books.

The practical resources are books that give you ideas for your ministries. They will help you develop your Sunday school, give you guidelines for teacher-training meetings, and offer you ideas for learning games and activities. These books are most often published by Group Publishing, Gospel Light Publications, and Standard Publishing. You can usually find lots of practical resources at your local Christian bookstore.

How do I get my church to consider children's ministry to be important?

Unfortunately many people believe that real spiritual teaching and learning don't begin until a child reaches the teenage years. Thus, in many churches the youth ministries and adult ministries get far more attention than the children's ministries. But that doesn't mean there's no hope for raising the visibility of the children's ministry.

● **Raise your church's awareness.** Think about how you can market the children's ministry to your church's congregation. How can you get the word out about the important work the children's ministry does? Develop a plan to intentionally use your church newsletter to broadcast news about the children's ministry. Don't use it just to report your needs; use it to tell about special events and fun activities your children are involved in.

● **Expose church leadership to your ministry.** Give your church leadership, including your pastor, a tour of your children's ministry in action. You may be surprised at what they don't know. Ask for time during your church's worship services to promote children's ministry. If your church has a youth

Sunday that is usually devoted to the youth ministries, ask that the children's ministries be included in the next one. Invite teachers to talk about their experiences. Invite children to talk about their experiences in the children's ministry. Show slides or video footage of special times from your children's ministry.

● **Set up an information station.** Ask permission to set up a children's ministry information station in a visible area of your church building. This can serve two purposes, first as a place visitors come with questions about children's ministry and second as a place to highlight special events and help all the members of your church understand your children's ministry.

● **Make presentations.** If your church offers adult education on Sunday mornings, use that opportunity to make presentations to adults about the children's ministry.

How do I get my pastor to address kids' needs from the pulpit?

● **Be sensitive to your pastor's agenda.** First, let's address this from the pastor's perspective. Many pastors work months, even years, in advance in planning their sermon schedules, or they follow a prescribed plan based on the church year. It can be difficult for a pastor to move from that plan to address specific needs of kids or the children's ministry in a sermon.

● **Raise your pastor's consciousness.** However, you can work on raising your pastor's consciousness about the needs of kids by keeping him or her apprised of all that's happening in your ministries. If something happens that you think would make a good sermon illustration, pass it on to your pastor. As you do this, your pastor will begin to consciously use appropriate illustrations about kids and the importance of the children's ministries. Work to develop a good relationship with your pastor. If he or she respects the person who represents the children's ministry, he or she will respect the ministry.

● **Make your expectations realistic.** Sometimes children's pastors are frustrated with their senior pastors because they won't continually use the pulpit to discuss the volunteer needs of the children's ministry. Perhaps children's pastors should see this pastoral reluctance as a call to rethink this strategy.

This week's sermon

**Is Heaven
Better Than
Walt Disney World?**

GLASBERGEN

"Our children's pastor thinks I should speak more to the children."

First, desperate pleas from the pulpit rarely work. The people who do respond are often not reliable and often don't become long-term children's ministry workers. Second, if all people ever hear from the pulpit is how needy the children's ministry is, why would they ever want to work there?

● *Develop clever announcements.* Work with your pastor to develop positive, upbeat announcements and presentations. Talk about how wonderful it is that God has given your church all these kids. In order to take advantage of this blessing, you need more people to teach children about Jesus. Pastors will be much happier delivering this message than one that says you will not have a fifth-grade boys class unless someone volunteers immediately. People will listen to what your pastor says, so make sure he or she is delivering the message you want the congregation to hear.

How should I respond to those who think children's ministry is glorified baby-sitting?

● *Education.* Work to educate these people about what is really happening in your children's ministry programs. But first make sure your children's programs are more than glorified baby-sitting.

● *Cast your vision.* Work on learning how to cast vision. Help the people who are not involved in your ministries understand why your ministries exist and what you hope to accomplish through them. Then show them evidence of your accomplishments. Talk continually about the results you see in the kids you serve. Talk about the spiritual growth and knowledge they gain because they are part of your church's children's ministries.

● *Share information.* Do everything you can to show the people in your church what is happening in your ministries. Offer to give tours of the children's areas to new members so they can glimpse all that's being accomplished there. Make good use of pictures, slides, and videos to help different groups in your church understand the eternal importance of what is being done in your children's programs. Help your church leaders to understand the vital necessity of your children's programs so they, too, can be advocates for your ministries with those people who see it only as baby-sitting.

But remember: No matter how hard you try to cast the vision, there will always be people who cannot catch it or who refuse to catch it. Don't worry about those people. Invest your time and energy in the people who have begun to glimpse the power of ministering to children.

How do I create a vital children's ministry with limited resources and personnel?

● *Develop a core group of children's ministry supporters.* Gather the people who have the same vision for children's ministry in your church that you do. Begin to meet together to pray for God's direction for the ministry. Then as you feel you are discerning God's wishes for your church and its ministry to children, begin to plan and dream of what you can do. Remember that you won't be able to do everything you want to do at once.

● *Work to determine priorities.* Determine what type of ministry will meet the needs of your church and community. Then study your monetary and personnel resources to decide how much you can do. Plan carefully so that kids are provided with an excellent ministry, no matter how small.

● *Plan and pray.* Look toward next year to begin to plan ways to expand the ministry you have already started or to determine the next ministry for children you should invest in. Continue to ask God to provide the money and the people to make your ministries fruitful.

Don't try to do too much at once. Ask God for direction, and then set your priorities accordingly.

What do I need to know about the law to protect myself and the church?

● **Know what the law says about hiring and supervising volunteers.** Know the laws in your state or province governing the hiring and supervision of volunteers who work with minors. In most states your church can be held liable for damages if you are proven to have been negligent in either the hiring or supervision of volunteers.

Don't think these laws are not applicable to you because these people are volunteers rather than employees. In the eyes of the law, any time you enlist a volunteer to serve, you are hiring him or her. Many state laws hold your church liable for the actions of a volunteer if you knew or should have known that the volunteer should not be working with minors and you continued to employee the volunteer. This is one reason screening your ministry volunteers is so important.

The other part of the law in most states holds your church liable for damages resulting from the improper supervision of your volunteers. This is one reason it is so important to establish policies and procedures for your children's ministry volunteers. And you must inform them of these policies once you have created them. These policies should include but are not limited to policies on diapering, taking children to the restroom, touching, dealing with accidents, and field trips.

● **Check with your insurer.** Check with your church's insurer to find out what it recommends in terms of child safety policies and volunteer screening. The insurer will be able to tell you about the liability laws in your state and how they have been interpreted by the courts.

● **Interview other churches.** You can learn from what other people have already done by talking to other churches in your community about their safety policies and procedures. If your church has a lawyer who is consulted on routine legal issues, talk to him or her about how to avoid liability and negligence.

Should our church have an AIDS policy?

Many churches have developed AIDS policies, including guidelines for dealing with HIV-infected children who become part of your ministries.

Creating these guidelines is complicated by several factors. First, churches do not have to be told if there is an HIV-infected child in their midst. And if the parents or caregivers do choose to tell you that their child is HIV-infected, you can tell only the people they give you permission to tell. Confidentiality laws exist. Second, despite all the publicity AIDS has received in past years, many people still operate under misconceptions about how one becomes infected. Many people still avoid and fear casual contact with someone who is HIV-positive.

- ***Have a plan ready before you need it.*** It's best to develop a plan before you are faced with this situation than when you are in the midst of it and emotions are running high. Check with other churches in your area to learn their AIDS policies. Check with local daycare centers and nursery schools to see how they deal with children who may be HIV-positive.

- ***Take action to prevent the spread of all disease.*** Ask nursery workers to wear rubber gloves when changing diapers. Make sure hand washing is part of the routine as well. Don't allow a child who is visibly ill into your nursery or classrooms, and let parents know that this is church policy.

Watch for biters in your preschool classrooms. If a child chronically bites others, talk with parents about ways to prevent this behavior, or remove the child from the classroom.

Have a supply of rubber gloves available to all your volunteers. They may need them as they deal with bloody noses or cleaning up vomit.

- ***Always act with love and compassion.*** Any child or adult who comes to your church and tells you he or she is HIV-positive should be welcomed and treated with love and compassion. These people should be treated as all other people are treated. You cannot become infected with AIDS through casual contact, and the support of the church is crucial in the lives of people who are infected.

Quick Relief for
Teacher Training

Quick Relief for Teacher Training

Use this one-hour training session to help your volunteer teachers learn more about becoming effective teachers of children in the church. Help to make this time enjoyable by serving refreshments. Focus on developing relationships with the teachers in your group. Listen closely to discover the ways in which they feel inadequate or insecure so that you can offer encouragement and training. Affirm their strengths. Use this time to discover how you can meet your teachers' needs with additional training, encouragement, prayer, resources, or other methods.

Objectives
Your teachers will
- discover obstacles to being better teachers,
- find the answers to their most pressing questions about teaching children, and
- discover that God can help them be better teachers of children.

Supplies
- one copy of *Quick Relief for Sunday School Teachers* (Group Publishing, 1998) for each teacher
- Bibles
- markers
- newsprint or poster board
- paper dolls that have been cut out
- masking tape
- paper and pencils

Preparation
Before the session, prepare three signs on newsprint or poster board. Hang them on three different walls of your meeting area. On one sign write, "Questions About Classroom Procedures"; on the second sign write, "Questions About How Kids Learn the Bible"; and on the third sign write, "Questions About Classroom Relationships."

Getting Started

Greet teachers as they arrive. When the group has assembled, form groups of no more than four. Give each group markers and a paper doll big enough to write words and phrases on.

Say: **Most of the time you hear what other people think a church teacher of children should do and be. Now you're going to have a chance to express your ideas. In your group, describe the perfect teacher of children. What would this person do and say? After you've talked about several characteristics, use your markers to write the characteristics on the paper doll. When you're finished, have someone in your group tape the doll to the wall in the front of the room.**

Give the groups several minutes to complete the project. When all the groups have taped their dolls to the wall, gain everyone's attention, and ask each group to talk about its vision of the perfect teacher of children in the church. Dig deeper into their answers by asking questions such as:

● Why did you choose that characteristic?

● Why would that characteristic make someone a good teacher of children?

After all the groups have shared their ideas, say: **Take a couple of minutes to think about the characteristics that we've shared. Choose three or four that you think you have. Then choose three or four characteristics that you'd really like to have. Find a partner, and talk about the characteristics you have and the characteristics you'd like to acquire.**

Give the volunteers three or four minutes for this discussion. Then say: **None of us is perfect, and none of us teaches children perfectly. But we can improve. One of the things that can stand in the way is not knowing the answers to some basic questions about teaching kids the Bible. Let's explore some of those questions and see if we can discover answers we can use the next time we teach children.**

Digging In

Direct your teachers' attention to the three signs hanging on the walls. Say: **Many questions volunteer teachers have about teaching children can be placed in one of these three categories. Their questions deal with how to work with kids in a classroom, how to specifically teach kids about the Bible, and how to build relationships with kids.**

Think about your questions about working with kids. Then decide what category your questions fall in. Your questions may fall in more than one category, but try to choose the category that describes most of your questions about teaching kids, then go and stand by that sign.

When all the teachers are standing by a sign, give each teacher a copy of *Quick Relief for Sunday School Teachers*, a pencil, and paper. If more than five teachers are standing by one sign, have them form two or more groups. If there is a category that no one chose, that's OK. That just means they have no questions about that area of teaching children and are concentrating on the areas in which they need help.

Say: **In your book you will find questions and answers divided according to the categories you chose from. In your group, read through the questions that correspond to your category. Pick the five questions and answers that are of the most concern to your group. Discuss them. Add to the answers, if you like, and then devise a way to present the material from your section to the rest of the group. For example, you could choose a spokesperson from your group to present the material, or you could create a skit to present the material.**

Give the groups about twenty-five minutes to complete this assignment. As they are working, visit each group, listen to the participants' discussions, and answer any questions they might have. After the groups have finished their assignments, gather them into one large group. Have each group present its material to the rest of the class. Encourage those presenting the material to answer questions from the rest of the class. After the presentations, ask:

● **What question and answer was most helpful to you as a volunteer teacher? Why?**

● **What will you try to do differently with your class because of what you learned here?**

Closing

Ask teachers to rejoin the groups of four they were in at the beginning of the session. Give each group a Bible and one of the following Scripture passages: Psalm 46:1; Psalm 54:4: Psalm 118:6, 7; and Psalm 124:8. If you have more than four groups, it's OK if more than one group has the same passage. If you have fewer than four groups, give one group more than one passage.

Say: **Look up the Bible passage, and answer the following questions.**

● **What kind of help does God offer?**
● **Why is God's help important and valuable?**
● **How could you use God's help in your work with children in the church?**

After groups have studied their passages, ask them to share some of their responses with the class. Say: **When we teach a class of children in the church, we never do it alone. God is always with us. God is there to help us with our preparation. God is there to help us with our attitudes. God is there to help us with discipline and teaching methods. Really, it is God's job to teach the kids. It is our job to be the willing helpers.**

Direct the class' attention back to the characteristics of good teachers. Say: **As we seek to become more effective teachers in the church, we can ask God's help in developing these characteristics. Let's close in prayer. For our prayer each of us will read one of the characteristics written on the paper dolls, and we'll continue reading until we've mentioned all of the characteristics.**

Begin your prayer by saying: **God, thank you for the opportunity to teach children about you. Thank you for promising to help us. Please help us to develop these characteristics. We want to develop...**

Have each teacher read one of the characteristics from the paper dolls. Continue until all the characteristics have been mentioned, then say: **Amen.**